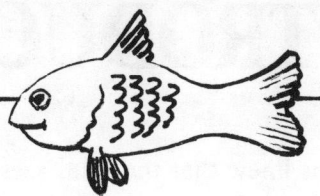 

Jesus
His Miracles

Matthew 8:23-34, 14:13-36, 15:32-39, 17:1-13, 24-27,
21:18-22, 28:1-20; Mark 4:36-41, 5:1-21, 6:30-52,
8:1-9, 11:12-14, 20-24, 12:13-17, 16:1-14;
Luke 8:22-40, 9:10-17, 24:1-49;
John 6:1-21, 20:1-23

by

Rebecca Daniel

illustrated by

Nancee McClure

A Christian Education Activity Book

Cover by Nancee McClure
Copyright © Good Apple, Inc., 1984
ISBN No. 0-86653-227-7
Printing No. 987654

Shining Star Publications
A Division of Good Apple, Inc.
Box 299
Carthage, IL 62321-0299

NOTE: The activities in this book were written using the King James Version of the Bible, so always use this version to solve the puzzles.

The purchase of this book entitles the buyer to duplicate the activity pages as needed for use by students in the buyer's classroom. Permission for any other use must be granted by Shining Star Publications.

All rights reserved. Printed in the United States of America.

INTRODUCTION

Jesus knew that the Pharisees were plotting to take His life, but He did not let that keep Him from carrying on the work God sent Him to do. He traveled widely with His disciples, teaching and performing miracles.

One day when Jesus and His disciples were in a boat at sea, there was a great storm. The disciples asked Jesus to save them. Jesus asked, "Why are ye fearful, O ye of little faith?" Then He calmed the sea. The men marvelled, saying, "What manner of man is this, that even the winds and the sea obey him!"

While Jesus was speaking to a great multitude one day, His disciples came to Him, saying, "Send the multitude away, that they may go into the villages, and buy themselves victuals." Jesus didn't send the people away in search of food. Instead He told them to sit down. He took the only available food, five loaves and two fishes, and looking to heaven, He blessed the food and broke it and gave it to His disciples. The disciples discovered that there was enough food to feed everyone! "And they did all eat, and were filled: and they took up the fragments that remained twelve baskets full. And they that had eaten were about five thousand men, besides women and children."

And after Jesus had sent the multitudes away, He went up into a mountain to pray. His disciples boarded a boat to go to the other side. The wind blew and the sea tossed the ship. "Jesus went unto them, walking on the sea." When the disciples saw Jesus walking on the sea, they thought it was a spirit and were afraid. Jesus spoke to them, "Be of good cheer; it is I; be not afraid." Peter offered to walk on the water to meet Jesus. Jesus told Peter to come. But when Peter saw the boisterous wind, he was afraid and began to sink. Peter cried, "Lord, save me." Immediately Jesus stretched out His hand and caught Peter. Jesus said to Peter, "O thou of little faith, wherefore didst thou doubt?" When they got into the boat, the storm stopped.

One day Jesus took Peter, James and John up onto a high mountain to pray. Jesus "was transfigured before them; and his face did shine as the sun, and his raiment was white as the light." Moses and Elias appeared and spoke to Jesus. A bright cloud overshadowed them and a voice out of the cloud said, "This is my beloved Son, in whom I am well pleased; hear ye him." The disciples were afraid and fell on their faces. Jesus touched them and said, "Arise, and be not afraid." On the way down from the mountain Jesus told His disciples not to tell anyone of the vision until "the Son of man be risen again from the dead."

Perhaps the most important miracle was the resurrection of the Lord. "And, behold, there was a great earthquake: for the angel of the Lord descended from heaven, and came and rolled back the stone from the door, and sat upon it . . . He is not here: for he is risen." Because of these miracles, people began to ask: "Is Jesus the Messiah?"

Shining Star Publication, Copyright © 1984, A division of Good Apple, Inc.

THE STILLING OF THE STORM

Matthew 8:23-27; Mark 4:36-41; Luke 8:22-25

Use the number code to solve this puzzle.
A=1, B=2, C=3, D=4, E=5, F=6, G=7, H=8, I=9,
J=10, K=11, L=12, M=13, N=14, O=15, P=16,
Q=17, R=18, S=19, T=20, U=21, V=22, W=23,
X=24, Y=25, Z=26

"1,14,4   2,5,8,15,12,4,   20,8,5,18,5
 And   behold   there

1,18,15,19,5 1 7,18,5,1,20 20,5,13,16,5,19,20
arose   a great   tempest

9,14   20,8,5   19,5,1 . . . 20,8,5,14   8,5
in   the   sea   and   __

1,18,15,19,5,   1,14,4   18,5,2,21,11,5,4   20,8,5
____   ____   _____   ____

23,9,14,4,19   1,14,4   20,8,5   19,5,1;   1,14,4
_____   ____   ____   ____   ____

20,8,5,18,5   23,1,19   1   7,18,5,1,20
_____   _____   _   _____

3,1,12,13."
_____

Name_____

Let the Scriptures help you solve this puzzle. Fill in the blanks with the correct words. Then place these words in the puzzle.

"But the ___ _____,

_____,What _____ of

____ is this, that _____ the _____

and the ___ _____ him!"

Matthew 8:27

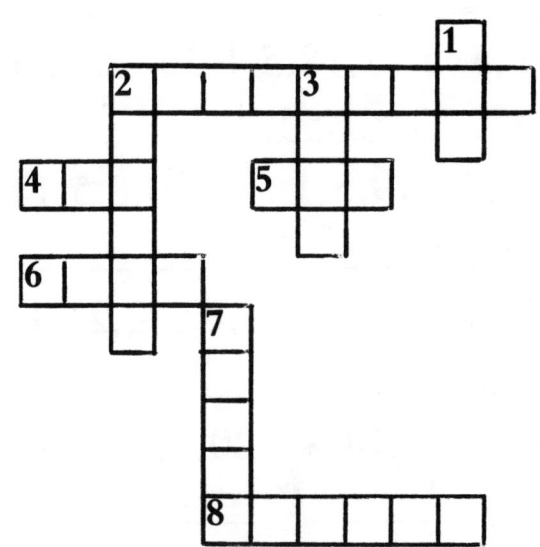

Below are three words from the Scriptures. They have been scrambled together. Can you unscramble these three words?

D A L O V E R U S S

ANSWER: "_____, _____ ___."

Name_____

DEMONS SUBJECT TO JESUS

Matthew 8:28-34; Mark 5:1-21; Luke 8:26-40

In each row of jumbled letters found below is a hidden word. To discover the secret message, circle the correct words and write them in the order they are found on the blanks below.

SECRET MESSAGE: "____ ____ __ __ __ ____ ____, ____, ____ ___ __ ___?"

```
H T I W A E H T J W H A T D H D E S A N
H A V E X T S M T E B J E C T D E M O E
T R M N I D K W E K T J E M D N E I D D
K D I T K E J T K T O M D C E I T K E E
T I D M O N T D O J E I M C E I D K K K
K D I M B I E I W M W I T H N L E W E K
M N N T H E E Y N U I I I E M D N I M M
J E S U S R B M N G E E T I U M N D F D
M N B O V E D D I M H H G T M N T H O U
M N G E A K E M D H K T S O N I E F K E
M M I K D N I M D N O F Z M N E K D I X
O M G B V E E H W T H W W G O D W I M B
```

Name_____

Shining Star Publication, Copyright © 1984, A division of Good Apple, Inc.

Finish these magic word squares by spelling words found in the Scriptures. The words must read down as well as across.

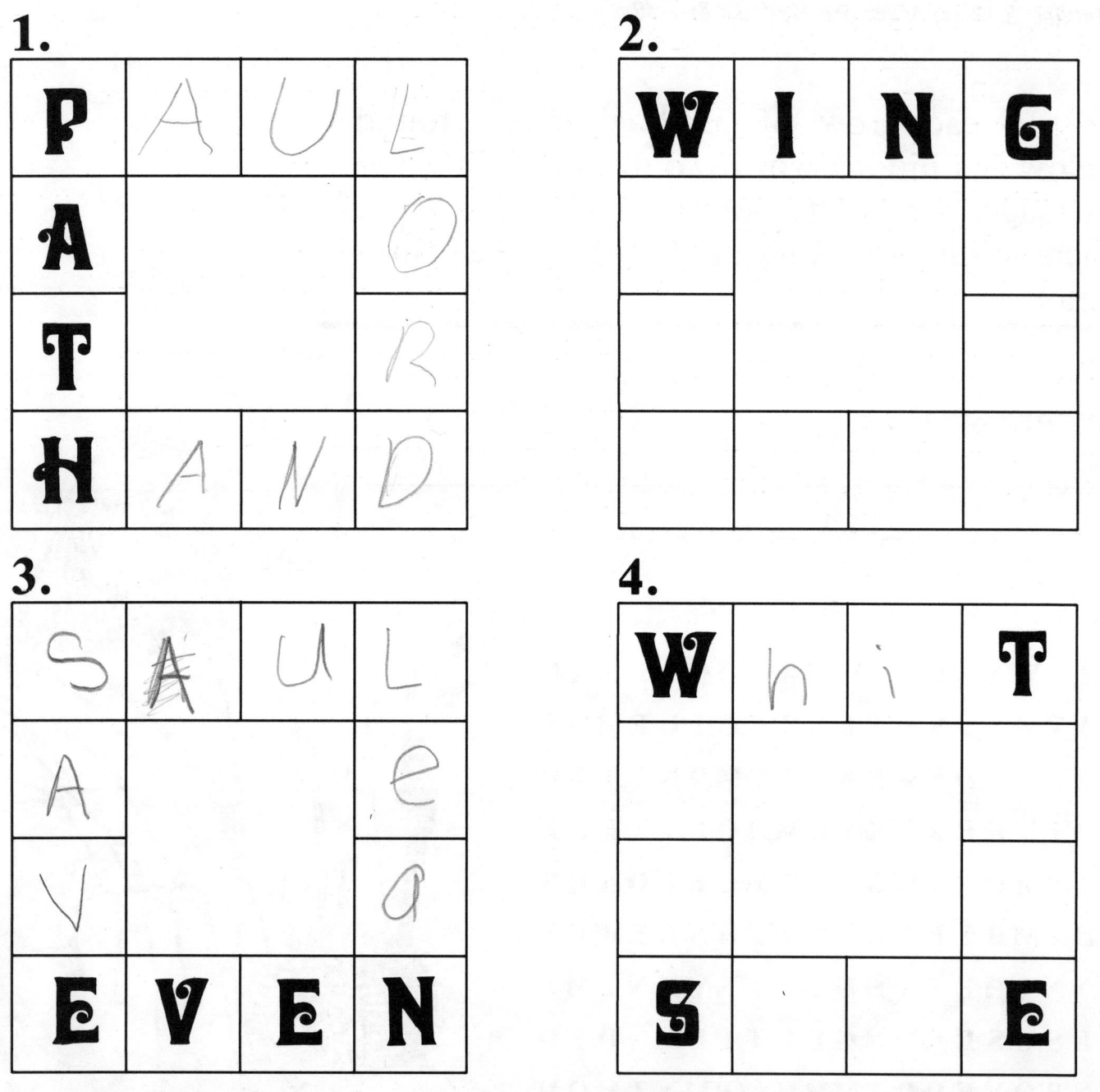

Make up your own magic word square using words found in the Scriptures.

Name_____

FEEDING FIVE THOUSAND

Matthew 14:13-21; Mark 6:30-44; Luke 9:10-17; John 6:1-14

Place the correct vowel in each blank to spell words and discover the secret message.

___

_n_ d_y wh_l_ pr___ch_ng _nd h__l_ng _n th_ c___ntrys_d_, J_s_s p_rf_rm_d _ m_r_cl_. Th_r_ w_r_ th___s_nds _f h_ngry p___pl_. _n_ sm_ll b_y h_d f_v_ l__v_s _f br__d _nd tw_ f_sh. J_s_s g_v_ th_nks _nd br_k_ th_ br__d _nd g_v_ _t t_ H_s d_sc_pl_s t_ g_v_ t_ th_ p___pl_. Th_r_ w_s m_r_ th_n _n___gh f___d t_ f__d th_ f_v_ th___s_nd p___pl_!

Name_____

Find and circle every word from the Scripture hidden in the letter maze below. The words may be written down, across or diagonally.

"They did all eat, and were filled: and they took up of the fragments that remained twelve baskets full."   *Matthew 14:20*

```
F T H E Y T H A Y T U E O
I R N T O O K O F T E P F
L B A S K E T S O U H B T
L A L G B A A N D K L E H
E S L E M S K T D F U L A
D A N D R E M A I N E D T
A T T O T F N T D W E R E
N R A K B H U T W E L V E
F I L L E B E B S A S K E
T W A E L V E Y L L B A T
```

Three letters in this message have been replaced with the letter *X*. Can you decode this message by filling in the correct letters?

"WX   XXVX   XXRX   BUT   FIVX

___   ____   ____   ____   ____

LOXVXS,   XND   TWO   FISXXS."

_____   ____   ____   _____

Name_____

JESUS WALKS ON WATER

Matthew 14:22-27; Mark 6:45-50; John 6:15-20

A	E	N
S	T	H
I	O	U

Use the code to solve the puzzle.

one evening as the sun
was setting the disciples
got into a boat to row
across the sea of Galilee
a storm came up. it was
soon dark and the wind
tossed the small boat.

Write the rest of the story in code.

Name_____

Begin in the upper left-hand corner and end in the lower right-hand corner. Find a path through the letters that spells a message. You must move across or down. You may not move diagonally.

SECRET MESSAGE: "__ __   __ __   __;   __ __   __ __ __   __ __ __ __ __ __."

```
I T I T I I T
T I S I T T S T
I S I S O I I I
I B B I N S B S
N E E B E I E I
O B N O T A N B
B E N O T F O T
E N O T A R A I
N O T A F R A D
```

What word found in the Scriptures can you put in the middle that makes three-letter words of the letters going down?

A	A	A	P	S	E	T	I	O	B	A
K	E	E	T	T	G	E	S	L	Y	E

Name _____

O THOU OF LITTLE FAITH

Matthew 14:28-36; Mark 6:51,52; John 6:21

To discover the secret message, follow the directions carefully.

IFLFR MAHLFD LO MATK OH LNF MALFR
___ ___ ___ ___ ___ ___

LO WFFL JFSUS. JFSUS LOTD IFLFR LO
___ ___ ___ ___ ___ ___

COWF OUL OE LNF SNPI. IFLFR MATKFD
___ ___ ___ ___ ___ ___

OH LNF MALFR UHLPT LNF MPHD BTFM
___ ___ ___ ___ ___ ___

AHD IFLFR MAS AERAPD. IFLFR BFGAH
___ ___ ___ ___ ___

LO SPHK AHD NF CATTFD LO JFSUS.
___ ___ ___ ___ ___ ___

JFSUS SLRFLCNFD OUL NPS NAHD AHD
___ ___ ___ ___ ___

CAUGNL IFLFR.
___ ___

Change all the T's to L's.
Change all the L's to T's.
Change all the H's to N's.
Change all the N's to H's.
Change all the E's to F's.
Change all the F's to E's.
Change all the W's to M's.
Change all the M's to W's.
Change all the I's to P's.
Change all the P's to I's.
The other letters are correct.

"COME."

Name _____

Unscramble the words below and write the secret message.

USJES ASID OT ETPER, "O HTOU FO
Jesus _said_ _to_ _Peter,_ _"O_ _thou_ _of_

TTLILE TIFAH, ERERWHFO SIDDT UOTH
little _faith,_ _wherefore_ _didst_ _thou_

TODUB?" EHWN ETHY MCAE OINT ETH
doubt?" _When_ _they_ _came_ _into_ _the_

PISH, ETH DNWI EPPSTOD GWOBLIN.
ship, _the_ _wind_ _stopped_ _blowing._

Draw a continuous line from letter to letter, going left, right, up or down. You may not move diagonally. When you finish, the letters should form a sentence. You must decide where to begin.

ANSWER: "THOU ART THE SON OF GOD."

S	O	F	G	O	D
E	N	O	T	H	O
H	T	T	R	A	U

Name_____

COMPASSION ON THE MULTITUDE

Matthew 15:32-34; Mark 8:1-9

Find the path through the maze. Color the path. To discover the message, write the letters in the order they are found.

SECRET MESSAGE: _ _ _ _ _ _

_ _ _ _ _ _   _ _ _   _ _ _ _ _

_ _ _ _ _ _   _ _ _ _ _ _

Name_____

To discover the secret message, write every other letter moving clockwise around the circle. You must decide where to begin.

SECRET MESSAGE: "_ _____ _____ __ ___ _____."

SECRET MESSAGE: "_ ____ ___ ____ ____ ____ _____."

(Circle 1 letters, clockwise): ·H·E·E·C·M·O·U·M·L·P·T·A·I·S·T·S·U·I·D·O·E·N·I·O·H·N·A·T·V·

(Circle 2 letters, clockwise): ·W·M·A·L·W·L·A·N·Y·O·F·T·A·S·S·E·T·N·D·N·T·G·H·I·E·W·

Make up your own circle puzzle using the Scriptures.

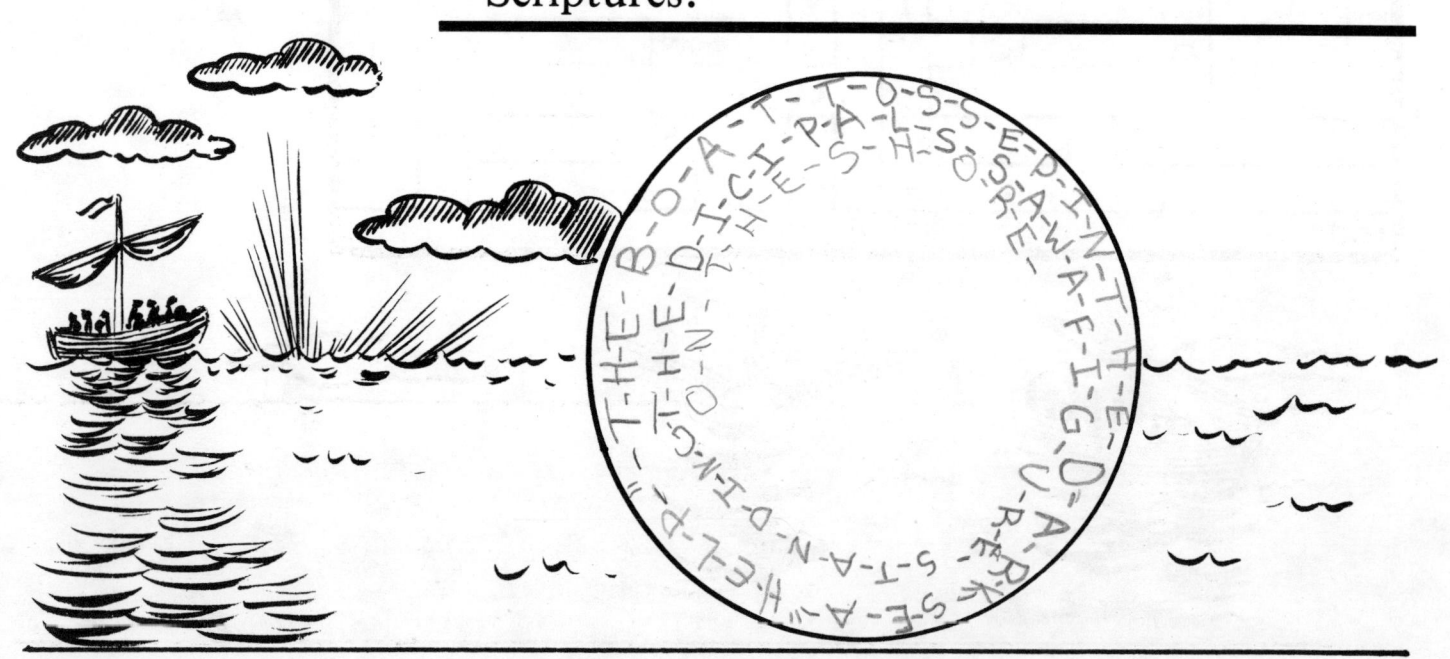

(Circle puzzle letters): ·T·H·E·—·B·O·A·T·—·T·O·S·S·E·D·—·I·N·—·T·H·E·—·D·I·C·I·P·A·L·S·—·S·H·O·S·R·E·—·A·—·F·I·G·D·U·R·R·K·S·E·A·—·S·T·A·N·D·I·N·G·—·O·N·—·T·H·E·—·P·

Name _____

Shining Star Publication, Copyright © 1984, A division of Good Apple, Inc.

A B C D E F G H I J K L M N O P Q R S T U V W X Y Z

SEVEN LOAVES AND FISHES

Matthew 15:35-39; Mark 8:7-9

To discover the secret message, write the letter of the alphabet that comes before each letter found below.

IF UPME UIF QFPQMF UP TJU EPXO PO
HE TOLD THE PEOPLE TO SIT DOWN ON

UIF HSPVOE. IF UPPL UIF TFWFO
THE GROUND HE TOOK THE SEVEN

MPBWFT BOE GJTIFT BOE HBWF UIBOLT
LOAVES AND FISHS AND GAVE THANKS

BOE CSPLF UIFN BOE HBWF UIFN UP
AND ____ ____ ____ ____ ____ ____

IJT EJTDJQMFT UP QBTT PVU UP UIF
____ ____ ____ ____ ____ ____ ____

QFPQMF.
____

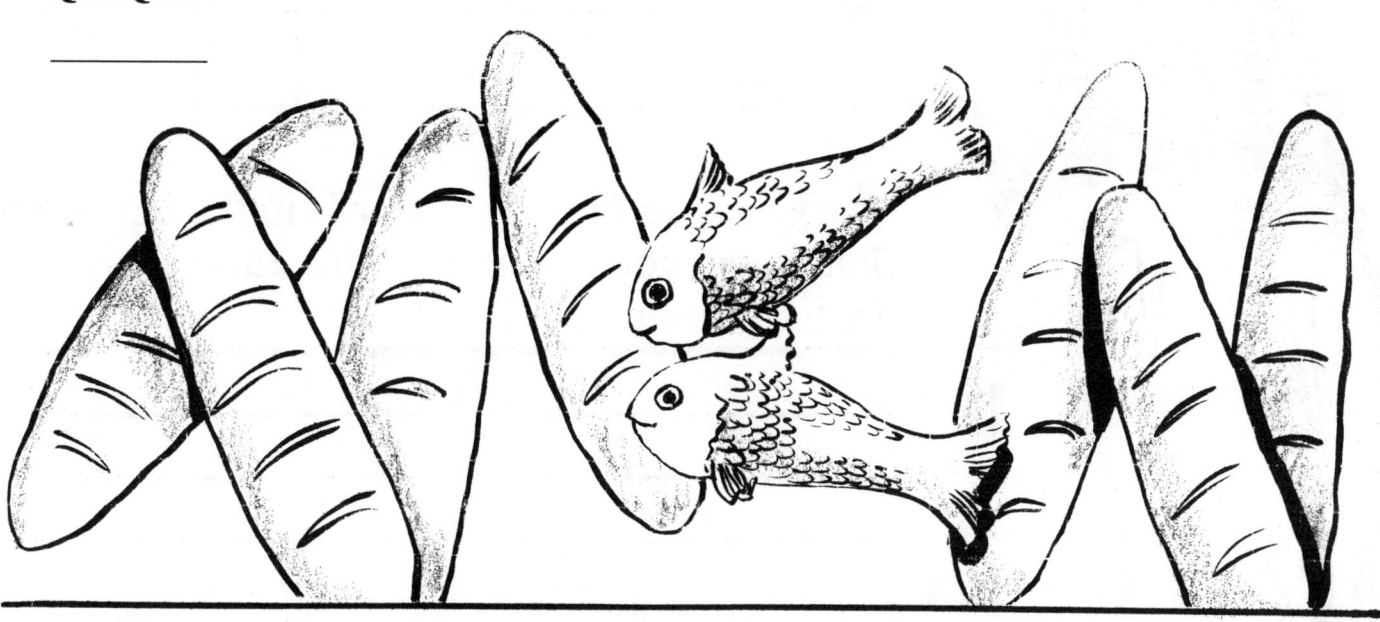

Name_____

Using the Scripture below, fill in the correct words in the crossword puzzle.

"And they did (3 across) (2 down), and (1 across) filled: and they took up of the broken (7 across) that was (4 down) (6 across) (5 down) full. And they that did (8 across) were four thousand men, (9 across) (1 down) and children."

Matthew 15:37,38

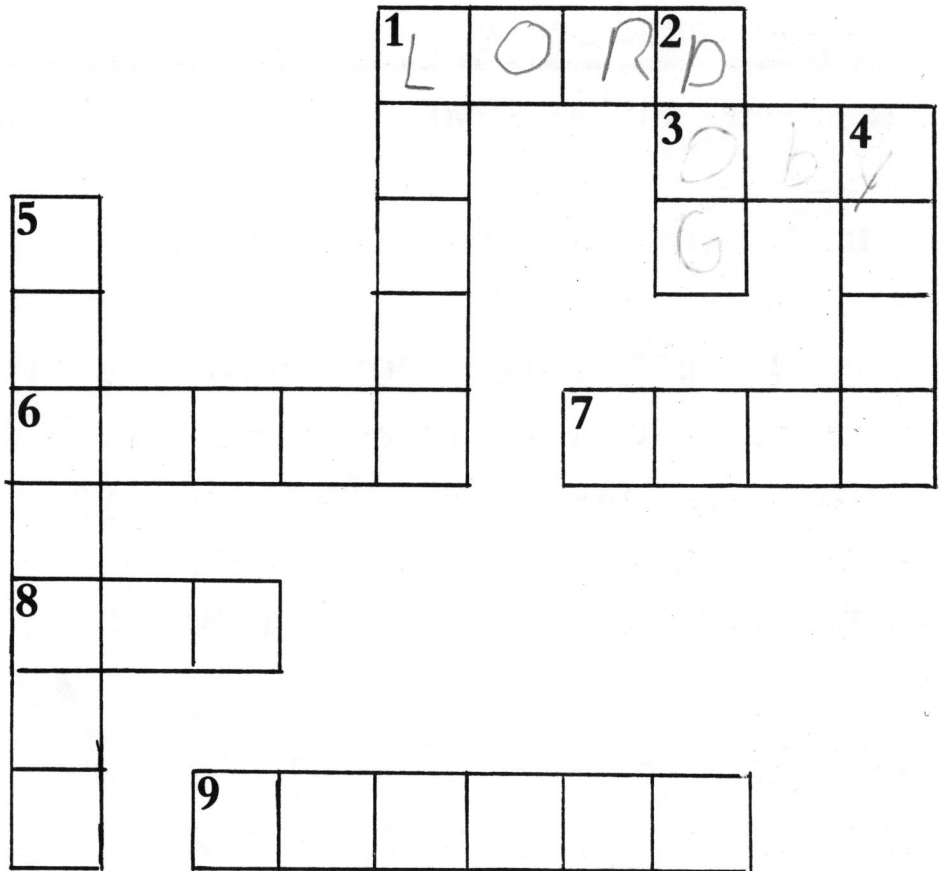

Can you find eight words in the Scriptures that have homonyms? Write each word and list its homonym.

1. _____ 5. _____
2. _____ 6. _____
3. _____ 7. _____
4. _____ 8. _____

Name _____

INTO THE HIGH MOUNTAINS

Matthew 17:1-6

To discover the secret message, follow the directions carefully.

SECRET MESSAGE: "_ _ _ _   _ _   _ _   _ _ _ _ _ _ _   _ _ _,   _ _   _ _ _ _   _   _ _   _ _ _ _   _ _ _ _ _ _ _;   _ _ _ _   _ _   _ _ _."

1.	T	H	I	S	K	A	N	G	A	R	O	O	B
2.	P	U	R	P	L	E	I	S	L	L	A	M	A
3.	C	O	L	T	M	Y	S	I	X	T	E	E	N
4.	B	E	L	O	V	E	D	T	H	I	R	T	Y
5.	C	A	M	E	L	Z	S	O	N	J	O	H	N
6.	A	M	Y	I	N	O	R	A	N	G	E	Z	A
7.	W	H	I	T	E	W	H	O	M	P	E	T	E
8.	A	I	H	O	R	S	E	A	L	L	E	N	A
9.	E	Z	A	M	S	E	V	E	N	T	Y	Z	E
10.	F	R	E	D	W	E	L	L	A	L	I	C	E
11.	O	Z	P	L	E	A	S	E	D	J	I	L	L
12.	F	O	U	R	H	E	A	R	S	A	R	A	H
13.	U	Y	E	Y	E	L	L	O	W	O	N	E	S
14.	S	Z	H	I	M	G	A	R	Y	P	I	N	K

Cross out the animal in lines 1,2,3,5 and 8.
Cross out the color in lines 2,6,7,13 and 14.
Cross out the number in lines 3,4,9,12 and 13.
Cross out the girl's name in lines 6, 10, 11 and 12.
Cross out the boy's name in lines 5,7,8,10, and 14.
Cross out the last letter in lines 1,6,8,9 and 13.
Cross out the first letter in lines 8,9,11,13 and 14.
Cross out all the z's.
Circle the words that are left to discover the secret message.

Name _____

Complete these word stars by spelling words found in the Scriptures. In each star, the words always have the same middle letter.

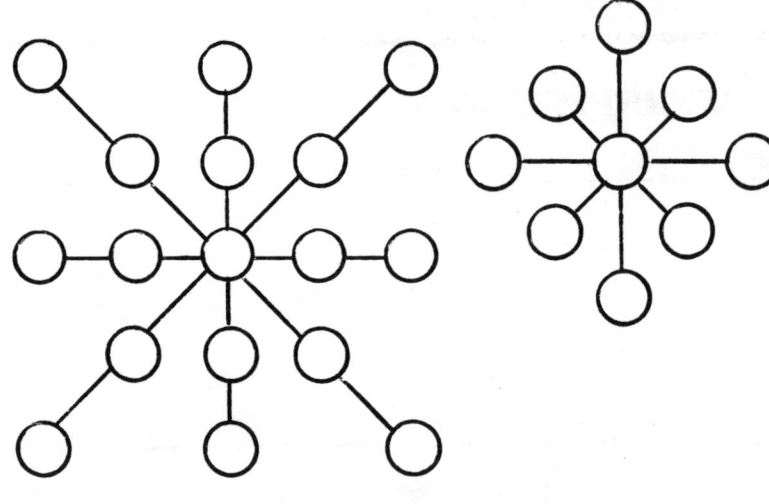

1.

2.

3.

Make up your own word star puzzle using the Scriptures.

Circle the first letter and then circle every third letter to discover the answer to this puzzle.

ANSWER: "_____ _____ __ _____ ____, ___ ____ ____ _____."

```
t j k h r u e m n y e w f i u e a f
l r t l g h o v b n w q t u y h w q
e m n i t r r m n f y u a c e c w e
e u y a b v n m c d q e w t y e i u
r y r e u i s t p o e w r q w e v n
a c x f i u r o p a y u i v b d
```

Name_____

ARISE, BE NOT AFRAID

Matthew 17:1-13

To discover the secret words, you will need your crayons. Color the spaces with one dot RED. Color the spaces with two dots YELLOW.

Name_____

Read each sentence. If the statement is correct, circle the letter under the letter *T*. If the statement is false, circle the letter under the letter *F*. To discover the secret message, fill in the blanks with the appropriate letters.

SECRET MESSAGE: $\overline{}\ \overline{}\ \overline{}\ \overline{}\ \overline{}$,
$\ \ \ \ 1\ \ 2\ \ 3\ \ 4\ \ 5$

$\overline{}\ \overline{}\ \ \overline{}\ \overline{}\ \overline{}\ \ \overline{}\ \overline{}\ \overline{}\ \overline{}\ \overline{}\ \overline{}$.
$6\ \ 5\ \ \ 7\ \ 8\ \ 9\ \ \ 1\ 10\ \ 2\ \ 1\ \ 3\ 11$

		T	F
1.	Jesus took Peter, James and John to a high mountain.	A	O
2.	Jesus took Peter, James and John onto a boat.	T	R
3.	Jesus' face did shine as the sun.	I	E
4.	His raiment was white as the light.	S	O
5.	Peter, James and John fell asleep.	Y	E
6.	There appeared Moses and Elias.	B	M
7.	Moses and Elias talked to Jesus.	N	W
8.	Peter said, "Lord, we must go."	A	O
9.	Peter said, "Let us make three tabernacles."	T	Q
10.	A voice said, "This is my beloved Son."	F	E
11.	The voice said, "I am well pleased with him."	D	A

Fill in the blanks to spell words found in the Scriptures.

a__	a___	__a__
__a__	__a___	__a___
__a__	__a___	a____
__a__	__a___	a__a__
__a__	a____	a__a___
a___	__a__	a____

Name_____

THE TRIBUTE MONEY

Matthew 17:24-27; Mark 12:13-17

Decode the secret message. All of the letters have been replaced with numbers. You must decide which letters stand for which numbers.

L=__ D=__ E=__ F=__ H=__ M=__
N=__ O=__ T=__ W=__ S=__ U=__

SECRET MESSAGE: "___ ___ ___ ___ ___ ___ ___ ___ ___ ___ ___ ___ ___ ___ ___ ___ ___ ___ ___ ___ ___ ___."

5,2,11,7   1,2   11,9,4,12,5,3   4,8,8,2,6,3
_____   __   _____   _____

7,9,2,10
_____

Name_____

To discover the secret message, follow the directions carefully.

$\overline{1}\ \overline{2}\ \overline{3}\ \overline{4}\ \overline{5}\quad \overline{6}\ \overline{7}\ \overline{8}\ \overline{9}\quad \overline{10}\ \overline{11}\ \overline{12}\ \overline{13}\ \overline{14}\quad \overline{15}\ \overline{16}$

$\overline{17}\ \overline{18}\quad \overline{19}\ \overline{20}\ \overline{21}\ \overline{22}\quad \overline{23}\ \overline{24}\quad \overline{25}\ \overline{26}\ \overline{27}\quad \overline{28}\ \overline{29}\ \overline{30}$.

$\overline{31}\ \overline{32}\ \overline{33}\ \overline{34}\ \overline{35}\quad \overline{36}\ \overline{37}\ \overline{38}\ \overline{39}\quad \overline{40}\ \overline{41}\ \overline{42}\quad \overline{43}\ \overline{44}\ \overline{45}\ \overline{46}\ \overline{47}$

$\overline{48}\ \overline{49}\ \overline{50}\ \overline{51}\quad \overline{52}\ \overline{53}\ \overline{54}\ \overline{55}\quad \overline{56}\ \overline{57}\quad \overline{58}\ \overline{59}\ \overline{60}\ \overline{61}\ \overline{62}\ \overline{63}$

$\overline{64}\ \overline{65}\ \overline{66}\ \overline{67}\ \overline{68}\quad \overline{69}\ \overline{70}\ \overline{71}\ \overline{72}\quad \overline{73}\ \overline{74}\ \overline{75}\ \overline{76}\ \overline{77}\quad \overline{78}\ \overline{79}$

$\overline{80}\ \overline{81}\ \overline{82}\quad \overline{83}\ \overline{84}\ \overline{85}\ \overline{86}\ \overline{87}\quad \overline{88}\ \overline{89}\quad \overline{90}\ \overline{91}\ \overline{92}\quad \overline{93}\ \overline{94}\ \overline{95}\ \overline{96}\ \overline{97}$

$\overline{98}\ \overline{99}\ \overline{100}\ \overline{101}\ \overline{102}$.

Put the letter *a* in spaces 30,37,54,59,70,91 and 99.
Put the letter *c* in space 58.
Put the letter *d* in spaces 9,39 and 68.
Put the letter *e* in spaces 2,11,13,27,29,32,42,57,72,76,95 and 101.
Put the letter *f* in spaces 19,43 and 48.
Put the letter *g* in spaces 17 and 61.
Put the letter *h* in spaces 22,26,41,51,53,56,62,69,87 and 94.
Put the letter *i* in spaces 20,23,38,44,49,78,80 and 96.
Put the letter *j* in spaces 1 and 31.
Put the letter *l* in spaces 8 and 67.
Put the letter *m* in spaces 73 and 83.
Put the letter *n* in spaces 24,75 and 79.
Put the letter *o* in spaces 7,16,18,65,74,84 and 89.
Put the letter *p* in spaces 10 and 90.
Put the letter *r* in spaces 14,45 and 97.
Put the letter *s* in spaces 3,5,21,28,33,35,36,46,50,82 and 102.
Put the letter *t* in spaces 6,12,15,25,40,47,52,55,63,81,86,88,93 and 98.
Put the letter *u* in spaces 4,34,60,66 and 85.
Put the letter *v* in space 71.
Put the letter *w* in space 64.
Put the letter *x* in space 100.
Put the letter *y* in spaces 77 and 92.

Name_____

A FIG TREE

Matthew 21:18-22; Mark 11:12-14, 20-24

Cross out one letter in each word to spell a new word and discover the answer to this puzzle. Then write your own message and put one extra letter in each word. Ask a friend to solve your puzzle.

THE DISCIPLES MARVELLED
HAT SHOW QUICKLY THE FIG
TREE WITHERED AWAY. JESUS
SAID, "...IF YE SHALL SAY
UNTO THIS MOUNTAIN, BE
THOU REMOVED, AND BE
THOU CAST INTO THE SEA;
IT SHALL BE DONE."

Name _____

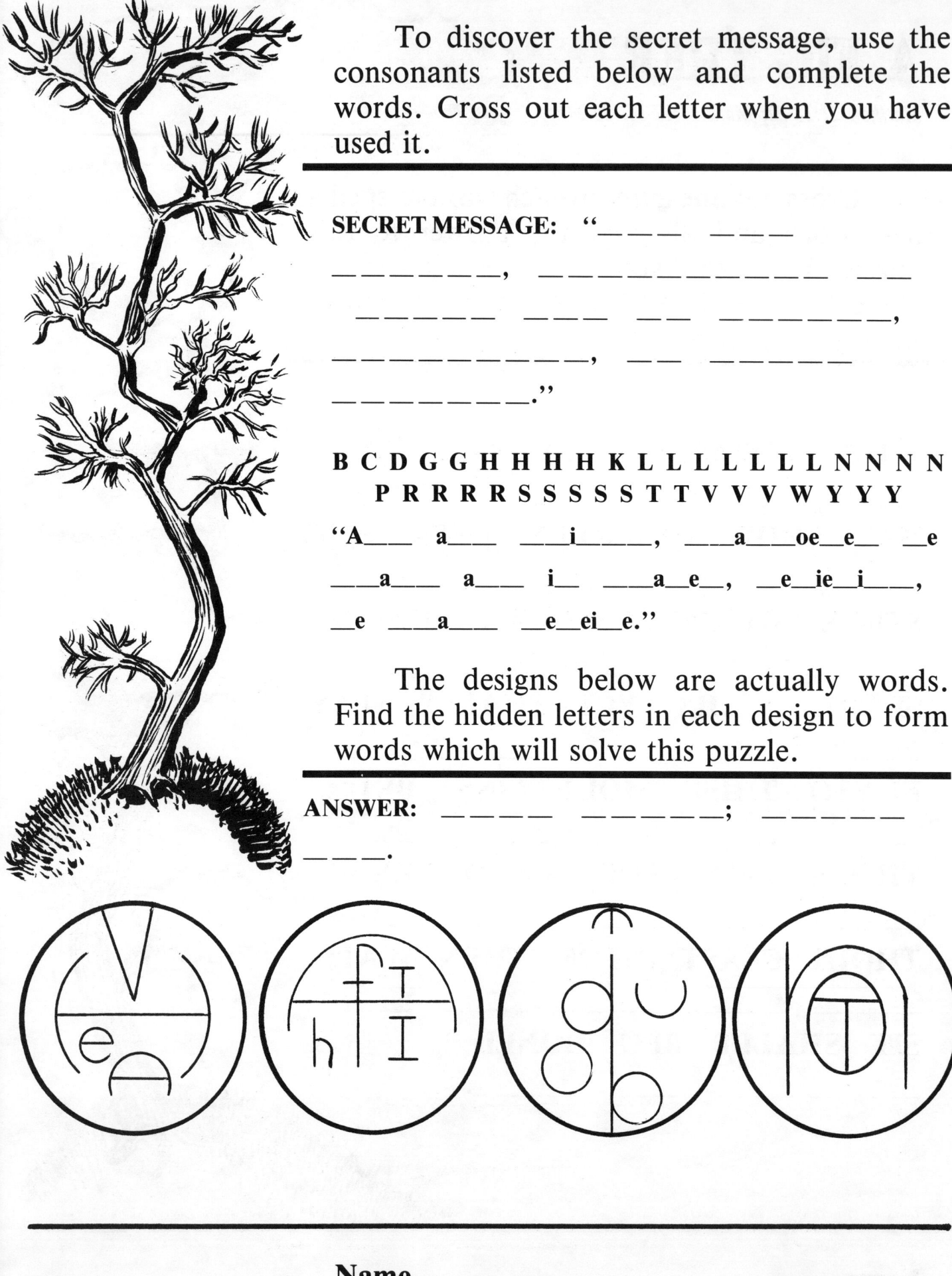

To discover the secret message, use the consonants listed below and complete the words. Cross out each letter when you have used it.

SECRET MESSAGE: "___ ___ _____, _____ __ _____ ___ __ _____, _____, __ _____ _____."

B C D G G H H H H K L L L L L L L N N N N
P R R R R S S S S S S T T V V V W Y Y Y

"A___ a___ ___i____, __a__oe_e_ _e __a__ a__ i_ __a_e, _e_ie_i__, _e __a__ _e_ei_e."

The designs below are actually words. Find the hidden letters in each design to form words which will solve this puzzle.

ANSWER: _____ _____; _____ ___.

Name_____

THE RESURRECTION

Matthew 28:1-8; Mark 16:1-14; Luke 24:1-49; John 20:1-23

To discover the secret message, follow each line and write the letters in the order they are found.

SECRET MESSAGE: "H E I S ___ ___ ___ ___ ___ ___ ___ : ___ ___ ___ ___ ___ ___ ___ ___ ___ ___ ___ ___ ."

Complete each word by adding one letter. The words are all found in the Scriptures. Then read down to discover the secret message.

SECRET MESSAGE: _ _ _ _ _   _ _ _
_ _ _ _ _   _ _ _

__or   __alilee
__arthquake   b__ing
he__ven   k__epers
__aiment   de__d
                    goe__h
pl__ce
rise__   __esus
Lor__   c__me
                    quickl__

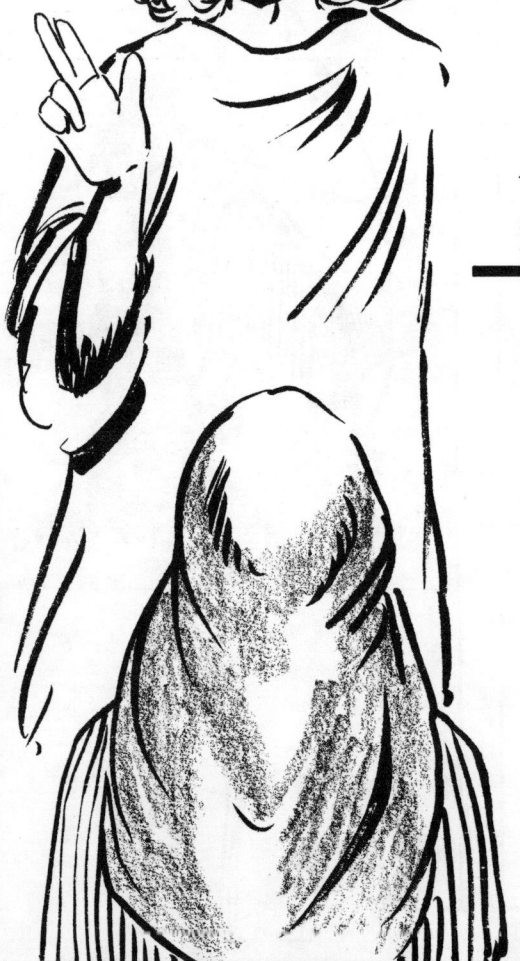

Can you spell eight words mentioned in the Scriptures using only the letters in the box found below?

F	R	N
S	I	H
T	D	W

1. _____   5. _____
2. _____   6. _____
3. _____   7. _____
4. _____   8. _____

Name _____

Shining Star Publication, Copyright © 1984, A division of Good Apple, Inc.

WITH YOU ALWAYS
Matthew 28:9-20

Can you read this rebus message? Let the Scriptures help you. Then write your own rebus message about this story.

Matthew 28:16,17

Name_____

All the vowels in the message below are incorrect. Replace the incorrect vowels with the correct vowels, and you will discover the secret message.

"Ga ya thorifuri, end taech ell netouns, beptuzeng tham on tha nemi if tha Fethur, end if tha Sun, end if tha Hily Ghast: Tuechung tham te ebsarva ell thengs whitseuvur a hevi cummendad yau: end li, a em woth yio elwey, avan intu tha and if tha wirld. Oman."

GO TEACH THE WORLD.

Name_____

REVIEW
Matthew 28

Begin in any circle and move along circles that are connected by a line. How many words found in the twenty-eighth chapter of Matthew can you spell? There are at least 16.

_____ _____ _____ _____
_____ _____ _____ _____

PRE AND POST-TEST

Read the statements below. If the statement is true, color the appropriately numbered spaces PURPLE. If the statement is false, color the appropriately numbered spaces GREEN.

1. Jesus performed many miracles but never in front of His disciples.
2. One day Jesus calmed a storm at sea.
3. One day Jesus took five fishes and two loaves of bread and fed five thousand men, women and children.
4. After five thousand people were fed, twelve baskets of food remained.
5. After Jesus sent the multitudes away, He went up into a mountain to pray.
6. Jesus walked on the sea to a boat where the disciples were.
7. Thomas asked Jesus if he could walk on the water, too.
8. Jesus took Peter, James and John up onto a mountain to pray.
9. Moses and Elias appeared and spoke to Jesus one day while He was with Peter, James and John.
10. One day Jesus told Peter to go fish in the sea for the money they needed to pay taxes.
11. Jesus told the disciples, "All things, whatsoever ye shall ask in prayer, believing, ye shall receive."
12. Jesus told His disciples, "Lo, I am with you alway, even unto the end of the world."

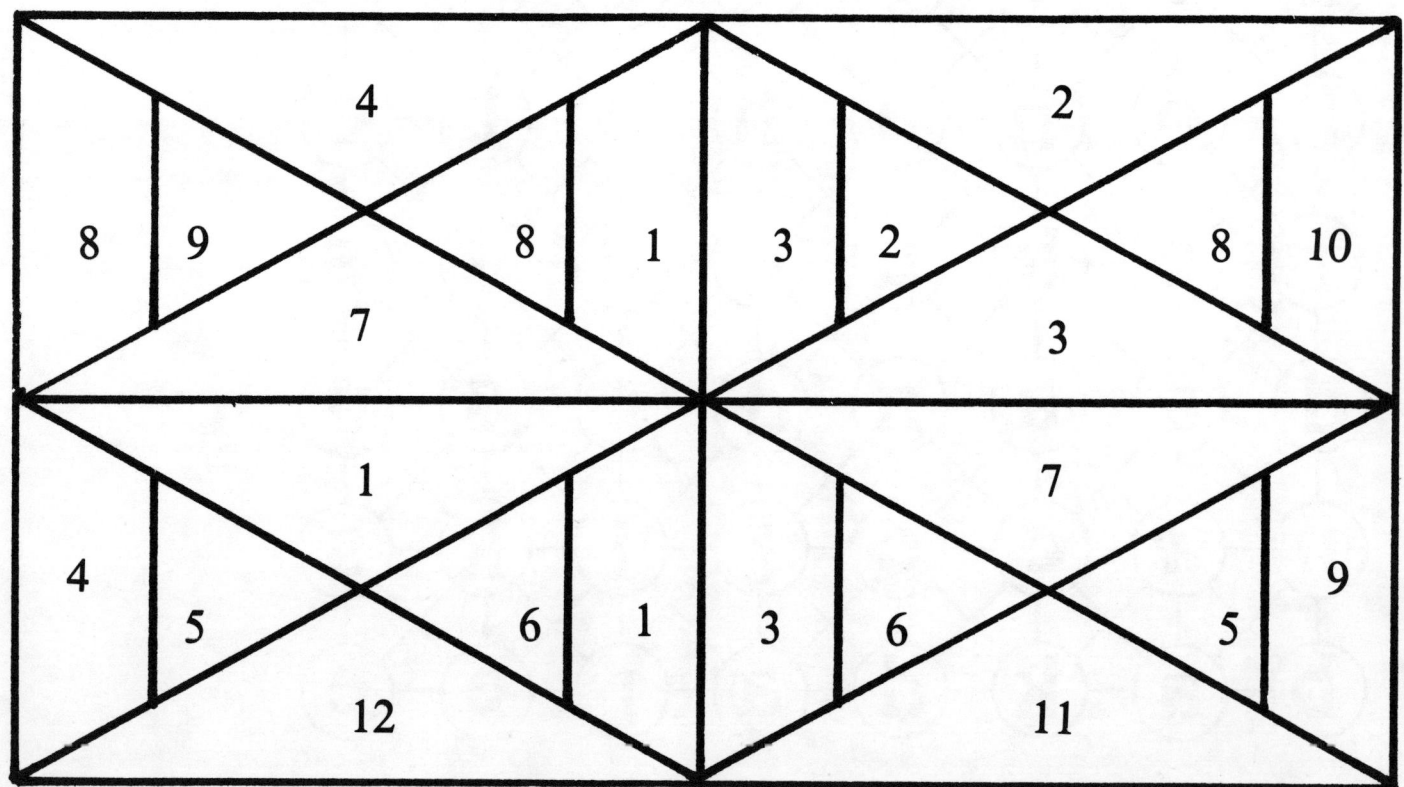

Name_____

ANSWER KEY

3. "And, behold, there arose a great tempest in the sea ... Then he arose, and rebuked the winds and the sea; and there was a great calm."

4. "But the men marvelled, saying, what manner of man is this, that even the winds and the sea obey him!"

   Across: Down:
   2. marvelled   1. men
   4. man   2. manner
   5. sea   3. even
   6. obey   7. winds
   8. saying

   "Lord, save us."

5. "What have we to do with thee, Jesus, thou Son of God?"

6.
   ```
   p a s s        w i n g
   a   i          e   o
   t   d          n   o
   h a v e        t o l d
   h e r d        w h a t
   a   o          a   h
   v   w          y   e
   e v e n        s i d e
   ```

7. One day while preaching and healing in the countryside, Jesus performed a miracle. There were thousands of hungry people. One small boy had five loaves of bread and two fish. Jesus gave thanks and broke the bread and gave it to His disciples to give to the people. There was more than enough food to feed the five thousand people!

8.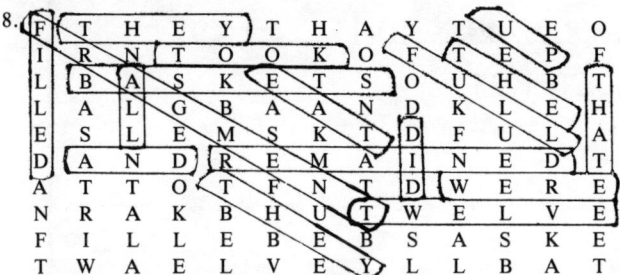

   "We have here but five loaves, and two fishes."

9. One evening as the sun was setting, the disciples got into a boat to row across the sea of Galilee. A storm came up. It was soon dark and the wind tossed the small boat.

10.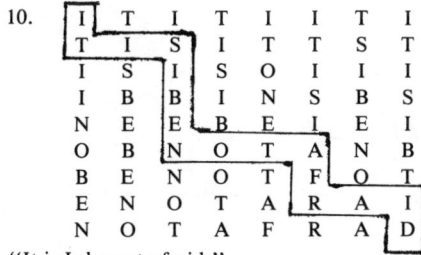

    "It is I; be not afraid."
    straightway

11. Peter wanted to walk on the water to meet Jesus. Jesus told Peter to come out of the ship. Peter walked on the water until the wind blew and Peter was afraid. Peter began to sink and he called to Jesus. Jesus stretched out His hand and caught Peter.

12. Jesus said to Peter, "O thou of little faith, wherefore didst thou doubt?" When they came into the ship, the wind stopped blowing.

    "Thou art the Son of God."

13. SEVEN LOAVES AND A FEW LITTLE FISHES

14. "I HAVE COMPASSION ON THE MULTITUDE."
    "I WILL NOT SEND THEM AWAY FASTING."

15. He told the people to sit down on the ground. He took the seven loaves and fishes and gave thanks and broke them and gave them to His disciples to pass out to the people.

16. Across:
    1. were
    3. all
    6. seven
    7. meat
    8. eat
    9. beside
    Down:
    1. women
    2. eat
    4. left
    5. baskets
    the, thee
    to, two, too
    brake, break
    all, awl
    meat, meet
    four, for
    sent, cent, scent
    so, sew

17. "THIS IS MY BELOVED SON, IN WHOM I AM WELL PLEASED; HEAR YE HIM."

18. 1. apart, spake, heard, pleased
    2. shine, white, Elias, voice or which
    3. him, six, his, did

    "They fell on their face, and were sore afraid."

19. MOSES   ELIAS

20. ARISE, BE NOT AFRAID.

    as, say, man, saw, had, all, and, save, said, came, also, that, dead, shall, arise, again, afraid, asked

21. "Lest we should offend them."
    L=5, D=3, E=2, F=8, H=9, M=10, N=6, O=4, T=7, W=1, S=11, U=12.

22. Jesus told Peter to go fish in the sea. Jesus said the first fish that he caught would have money in its mouth to pay their taxes.

23. The disciples marvelled at how quickly the fig tree withered away. Jesus said, "... if ye shall say unto this mountain, Be thou removed, and be thou cast into the sea; it shall be done."

24. "And all things, whatsoever ye shall ask in prayer, believing, ye shall receive."

    Have faith, doubt not.

25. "HE IS NOT HERE: FOR HE IS RISEN."

26. FEAR AND GREAT JOY
    in, it, first, his, did, I, is, with

27. "Then the eleven disciples went away into Galilee, into a mountain where Jesus had appointed them. And when they saw him, they worshipped him: but some doubted."

28. "Go ye therefore, and teach all nations, baptizing them in the name of the Father, and of the Son, and of the Holy Ghost: Teaching them to observe all things whatsoever I have commanded you: and lo, I am with you alway, even unto the end of the world. Amen."

29. sabbath, dawn, behold, great, earthquake, angel, Lord, and, rolled, back, in, fear, not, Jesus, seek, risen

30. true: 2,4,5,6,8,9,10,11,12
    false: 1,3,7

Shining Star Publication, Copyright © 1984, A division of Good Apple, Inc.

AWARD CERTIFICATE

This is to certify that

_____

has successfully completed a study of the miracles of Jesus. The Scriptures covered

Matthew 8:23-34, 14:13-36, 15:32-39, 17:1-13, 24-27, 21:18-22, 28:1-20; Mark 4:36-41, 5:1-21, 6:30-52, 8:1-9, 11:12-14, 20-24, 12:13-17, 16:1-14; Luke 8:22-40, 9:10-17, 24:1-49; John 6:1-21, 20:1-23.

_____
signature (teacher)

_____
signature (pastor)

_____
date